Movie Publicity Showcase Volume 5

Laurel and Hardy in "Sons of the Desert"

I. Joseph Hyatt

The intent of this book is to use the original press book in the same style and manner as it was used in 1933 to set the film into its historical perspective. The press book has been reproduced as closely as possible to the original with exceptions noted in the text.

To purchase books in quantity for fund raising, classroom use or to use as incentives email HVCScrapbook@aol.com.

ISBN: 1517198453
ISBN-13: 978-1517198459

DEDICATION

To all the people who worked on the films in front of and behind the cameras. To all the people who worked in the offices creating the publicity. To all the people that helped in the distribution and exhibition of this movie. To all the people working today to preserve and make available classic films to the public.

To the members of the Sons of the Desert, the Laurel and Hardy Appreciation Society, for helping to keep the films of Laurel and Hardy alive.

To my wife Mary who has put up with my old movie obsession all these years.

ACKNOWLEDGMENTS

"Sons of the Desert" is a 1933 American film comedy directed by William A. Seiter, produced by Hal Roach and starring Stan Laurel and Oliver Hardy. It also features Charlie Chase, Mae Bush, Dorothy Christy, and Lucien Littlefield. Ty Parvis sings "Honolulu Baby" by T. Marvin Hatley. It was partly based on an earlier two reel Laurel and Hardy silent comedy "We Fall Down" released in 1928. "Sons of the Desert" was released in Europe as "Fraternally Yours."

The movie is shown on Turner Classic Movies Channel in the US. Check listings at TCM.com for show times.

In the United States and Canada, at the time of this writing, "Sons of the Desert" is available as part of the 10 disc DVD set "Laurel & Hardy: The Essential Collection" from Vivendi Entertainment. In the United Kingdom and Europe "Sons of the Desert" is available in two collections, "Best of Laurel and Hardy" and "Laurel and Hardy: The Collection", both released by Universal Pictures UK. It is also available on separate discs. All of these can be found wherever you buy your movies and books.

The following press book reproduction will help bring you back to the film's 1933 release. There are no spoilers contained in this book. I hope you enjoy this book and the film.

I. Joseph Hyatt
September 29, 2015

INTRODUCTION FROM VOLUME 1
MOVIE PUBLICITY SHOWCASE: LAUREL & HARDY IN "SWISS MISS"

For many "old time" movie fans that grew up in the sixties and seventies, television gave us our first exposure to classic films. In a day before video tape recorders, cable, streaming, DVD, Blu-ray, and computers we considered ourselves lucky when one of our favorite movies was broadcast. With the exception of the CBS annual broadcast of "The Wizard of Oz" and stations such as New York's WOR that ran one movie (Million Dollar Movie) eleven times a week, an average movie would probably air twice in a five year period.

However there was an exception. A large one, mainly aimed for a children's audience. You could find movie series like "The East Side Kids/Bowery Boys", "Laurel and Hardy", "Abbott and Costello" and low budget horror movies weekly airing every Saturday. Under group titles such as "East Side Comedy" or "Chiller Theater" weekly showings of many of these favorites were more visible than the serious or classic films.

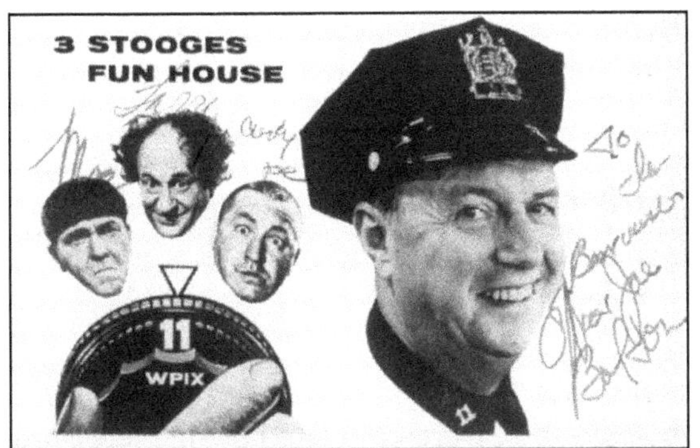

WPIX's Officer Joe Bolton presented the Three Stooges daily.

Chuck McCann with the Paul Ashley Puppets.

Early ad for Chuck McCann's daily show.

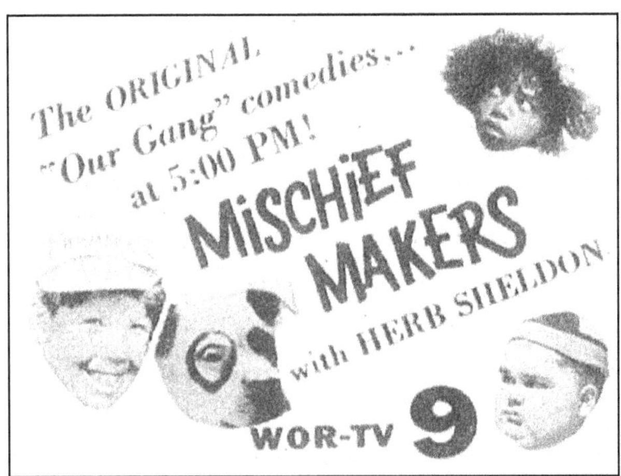

The Little Rascals/Our Gang were funny under any name.

Making the rounds of TV stations during this same period were a number of movie shorts collections, the most visible of these clusters being the Three Stooges, Laurel and Hardy and the Little Rascals/Our Gang. On many stations they were run with a live host. Chuck McCann, "Officer" Joe Bolton, Alan Swift and John Zacherley were hosts in the New York/New Jersey market. Other cities across the country had their own local hosts. Often these shows would broadcast Monday through Friday, and appear on the weekends as well.

Since we couldn't own a copy of the film as you can today, many of us tried to "capture" a bit of the emotions we felt by buying magazines, comics, toys, photos, and records with our favorite movie personalities. Sound tracks were recorded on our reel-to-reel audio tape recorders. Some of us even had a family home movie projector where you could buy a few minutes of older films and cartoons in 8mm silent (later sound) editions for a reasonable price (if we saved up our money and dad let us use the family projector). For most of us, a more professional film gauge was just an expensive dream.

Now collectables like movie posters, photos, and other movie memorabilia are very expensive. Back in the 1960's and earlier theaters and movie distributors would recycle posters, photos and movie campaign books until the films reached the end of their theatrical showings. Then these paper items would be disposed of. The suppliers (like National Cinema Service) either threw out or gave these mementoes to anyone who would clear their warehouse. Stores like Marc Ricci's Memory Shop in New York City and many more acquired much of this material by the truckload. Before these items were considered collectable (or even worthy of preservation) we could purchase some of these photos, lobby cards, and posters between $1 - $7 each in stores like these, or through mail order.

Today many posters sell in the 5 and 6 figures range. Pre-1940 material is the most expensive, since many of the paper items were donated (and recycled) for the war effort. Today it takes a collector with "deep pockets" to afford some of the original material.

For movie lovers and students of film one of these prize collectables is the movie campaign book. Originally campaign books, more commonly referred to as "press books", were circulated to theaters during the film's distribution. They were used so the movie exhibitor could pick out the posters that would fit his theater front and to chose pre-written articles and ads to run in newspapers within the theater's advertising budget.

Without trying, press books ended up documenting the choice of posters, banners, photos and other promotional items that were available for future generations. Radio ads and ideas for lobby displays, publicity articles, newspaper ad artwork, and general information about the film was also documented within its pages.

This series of books, starting with "Movie Publicity Showcase - Volume One - Laurel and Hardy in Swiss Miss", have been put together to allow people to understand what it was like to be a patron (or theater manager) when these films were originally presented. It is also a source for other film students, writers, or the movie enthusiast to read items (some fact- some Hollywood fiction at its finest) that were written to make an audience desire to be in the movie's audience.

Most of the press books in this series are presented as they were originally printed with two exceptions. A common size for these press books was approximately 12" x 18" in size. While full pages were used to represent the cover, back and poster pages, articles had to be separated and enlarged to make reading possible in this 8.5" x 11" book format. The synopsis covering the story (which included the ending) has also been eliminated. These synopsizes were not intended for use in publicizing the movie and give away the total story, including the ending.

Many archives and movie studios are now actively restoring and preserving the remaining film and advertising elements that still exist today.

Whenever a movie in this series is available, I hope that reading the original publicity material will encourage you to seek out the title. For information on the film's availability and other important information about the film's preservation, refer to the acknowledgement section in the front of this book.

INTRODUCTION TO VOLUME 5

MOVIE PUBLICITY SHOWCASE: LAUREL & HARDY IN "SONS OF THE DESERT"

"Sons of the Desert" is a 1933 American film starring Stan Laurel, Oliver Hardy, Mae Busch, Dorothy Christy, Charley Chase, and Lucian Littlefield. Produced by Hal Roach and directed by William A. Seiter, it was first released in the United States at the end of 1933 and is regarded as one of Laurel and Hardy's greatest films. In the United Kingdom, the film was originally released under the title "Fraternally Yours".

In 2012, the film was deemed "culturally, historically, or aesthetically significant" by the United States Library of Congress and selected for preservation in the National Film Registry.

The film opens at a meeting of Oasis 13, "the oldest lodge of the great Order of the Sons of the Desert", where members, dressed in tasseled fezzes and sashes, are singing "Auld Lang Sine". The "brothers" are directed to sit with one knock of the "Exalted Ruler's" gavel, then told about their annual convention in Chicago in a week's time.

"Down through the centuries of time in the history of this fraternal organization" they are told that no man has broken their sacred oath. They are given the oath, and both men attest that they will be in attendance. The position in which they received the oath involved crossing their arms and clasping the hands of the men on either side of them. The meeting is closed with the singing of "We Are the Sons of the Desert":

We Are the Sons of the Desert
By Frank Craven
We are the Sons of the Desert,
Having the time of our lives.
Marching along, two thousand strong,
Far from our sweethearts and wives, God bless them.
Tramp, Tramp, Tramp, the boys are marching,
And dancing to this melody.
Na Na Naa Na Na
Na Na Naa Naa Na Na Naa, [tune: Arabian Song *]
Sons of the Desert are we!

"Sons of the Desert" is a very enjoyable film. The original publicity material is reprinted here to place the film in context for the viewer, and to add to the enjoyment of watching a film made in 1933 with the advertising and exploitation that original audiences saw at the time of the movie's initial release.

A FURTHER NOTE: THE FILMS CLASSICS REISSUE

Film Classics (later Favorite Films) was a film distributor that specialized in movie reissues to theaters. It was formed in 1946 by Moe Kerman (of Astor Films, another distributor of reissued movies) along with J. J. Felder and Leo Seligman. They acquired the rights to redistribute "Sons of the Desert." Film Classics, a low budget corporation, utilized as much publicity from the original release campaign as possible.

Film Classics did change the posters for the film. New one sheets, inserts, and lobby cards were quickly produced. With bright colors and new arrangements, the posters used for the reissue gave a newer, more modern look than the original 1933 material. Toward the end of the book, some of these reissue materials are reprinted.

The audiences in the 1940's saw a slightly different publicity package on the theater fronts, however they saw the same "Sons of the Desert" that has been entertaining comedy enthusiasts for over 8 decades.

THE "SONS OF THE DESERT", THE LAUREL AND HARDY APPRECIATION SOCIETY

The "Sons of the Desert" is an international Fraternal organization devoted to the lives and films of comedians Stan Laurel and Oliver Hardy. The group takes its name from the lodge that Laurel and Hardy belonged to in the movie "Sons of the Desert.

In 1964, a few years after the book, "Mr. Laurel and Mr. Hardy", was published, author John McCabe formed a small group of Laurel and Hardy admirers, including Orson Bean, Al Kilgore, Chuck McCann and John Municino. McCabe created a mock-serious "constitution" that satirized the formalities of many social organizations. Stan Laurel endorsed and humorously revised the document. He also suggested that members might wear a fez or blazer patch with the motto "Two Minds Without a Single Thought." Founding member Kilgore created a logo with the motto in Latin (in the spirit of Laurel's dictum that the organization should have "a half-assed dignity" about it) as "Duae tabulae rasae in quibus nihil scriptum est" which translates (roughly) to: "Two blank slates on which nothing has been written").

The first public Sons of the Desert meeting was held in New York City in 1965. This group, the "Founding Tent", quickly inspired chapters in other United States cities, and in other countries. Members meet regularly to enjoy Laurel and Hardy movies in an informal atmosphere. Many chapters formed in the 1960s are still active today.

In addition to local and regional meetings, the Sons of the Desert holds international conventions, every two years since 1978. Most have been located in the United States but some have been held in other countries. There are also conventions held regularly in the United Kingdom and in Europe.

Information is available for those interested in joining the "Sons of the Desert" is available at the "Way Out West" tent's web site: http://www.wayoutwest.org/. Each local "tent" takes the name of a Laurel and Hardy movie. There are now chapters in eleven countries.

The front cover of the original 1933 "Sons of the Desert" Press Book.

Exhibitors CAMPAIGN BOOK

STAN LAUREL OLIVER HARDY

IN

"SONS OF THE DESERT"

Laurel and Hardy
in "Sons of the Desert"

Cut or Mat 608-E

• CAST •

STAN LAUREL
OLIVER HARDY
CHARLEY CHASE
MAE BUSCH
DOROTHY CHRISTY
LUCIEN LITTLEFIELD

•

DIRECTOR: WILLIAM A. SEITER

STORY AND CONTINUITY BY: FRANK CRAVEN and BYRON MORGAN

PHOTOGRAPHY BY: KENNETH PEACH

FILM EDITOR: BERT JORDAN

HISTORY: An original story for the screen by Frank Craven and Byron Morgan

Stan Laurel, Oliver Hardy and Charley Chase join forces in the new Laurel and Hardy feature-length laugh riot, "Sons of the Desert," coming soon to the . . . . Theatre. The boys are lodge "brothers" who duck their wives to have a carousing time at the annual convention. And do they have a time!

Cut or Mat 608-A

MEET THE PLAYERS

STAN LAUREL

Of a professional family, Stan Laurel, vacant-faced member of the stellar comedy team, Laurel and Hardy, is one of the more prominent of the screen comics who were schooled in English music halls. Like Charlie Chaplin, Laurel, as a boy, never knew a real home, living in trunks, dressing rooms, railroad stations and theatres and traveling with his parents' while they toured with various troupes of performers. Born in Ulverston, a small manufacturing community in England, Stan's education was a hit and miss affair, his mother teaching him at times when conditions would permit.

Cut or Mat 608-B

Laurel came to this country in 1910 with Fred Karno's show, the same organization that brought Chaplin to America. For nearly four years this troupe toured America and when it eventually disbanded, Stan went on the vaudeville stage. Later he was offered screen work with the Universal studios, and he divided his time between the stage and screen, preferring the former. At no time during this period did he command much attention and it was not until he joined Hal Roach studios in 1922 and shortly afterwards was teamed with Oliver Hardy that he clicked in a big way. Likewise, it was the merger that brought Oliver Hardy to screen fame after an uncertain career.

Contrary to his screen character, Laurel is one of the shrewdest, as well as one of the most brilliant, comics in the picture business. He is largely responsible for most of the scenarios he and his rotund partner interpret on the screen. Five feet, ten inches in height, Stan weighs 150 pounds. He is an accomplished athlete.

Mae Busch, Dorothy Christy and Laurel and Hardy in "Sons of the Desert"

Cut or Mat 608-F

OLIVER HARDY

Despite the handicap of being the fat boy of his neighborhood gang, Oliver Hardy, rotund member of the famous screen team of Laurel and Hardy, was the most popular lad of the group because he knew how to amuse and entertain the others. This talent, however, was not taken into consideration when his parents, who were non-professionals, decided upon a career for their bouncing off-spring.

Cut or Mat 608-C

Born and educated in Atlanta, Georgia, Oliver, or "Babe," as he is better known to his close associates, studied law at the University of Georgia. But the lure of the theatre was too strong, so Hardy tossed aside his cap and gown and began his career in the theatre following his graduation. Beginning at the lowest rung of the ladder, "Babe" successively served as doorman, bit actor, illustrated song singer and as a film extra before he joined the Hal Roach studios as a minor comic. It was not until he was teamed with Stan Laurel that he attained nation-wide recognition as a funster, both he and Stan Laurel winning stardom over night.

CHARLEY CHASE

Horatio Alger would have found in Charley Chase a worthy subject for one of his success stories. His rise from the streets of Baltimore, where he was born thirty-odd years ago, to stardom in screen comedies, reads like fiction.

Chase began his professional career as a song and dance actor. Landing in Hollywood on a vaudeville tour, he secured extra work at various studios and eventually secured regular employment in a film stock company. Later, he directed pictures and it was in this capacity that he was first employed at the Hal Roach studios. But word soon leaked out that Charley's efforts as a comedian for the company for which he previously worked were being acclaimed by exhibitors, and seeing starring possibilities in him, Roach induced Chase to resume his career as an actor. Soon he was starring in his own comedies.

Cut or Mat 608-D

His role in "Sons of the Desert" in support of Laurel and Hardy marks his initial appearance in a production other than his own since his advent as a star in his own right.

Charley is a tall, dapper fellow with a natural flair for comedy. He is a talented singer and dancer and is a master of pantomime. He is married and the father of two grown daughters. He rides horseback, flies, hunts and fishes.

HEARD ON THE LOT

With rare exception, the comedy team of Laurel and Hardy are never seen on the stage or heard over the radio. Not that the funster duo are prejudiced against this form of entertainment; to the contrary, they are great admirers of both branches of the amusement art. They have refrained from making footlight appearances and from talking into a "mike" because they believe that they owe sole allegiance to the motion picture industry as long as they are a part of it and that outside interests might detract from their studio work. On not more than two occasions have Laurel and Hardy deviated from the hard and fast rule they have laid down for themselves and these exceptions were for the cause of charity. The inimitable comics will soon be seen in their latest feature fun film, "Sons of the Desert," coming attraction at the . . . . Theatre.

•

"There's at least one at every party, club meeting or convention ever held." So declares Charley Chase in describing the character he portrays in support of Laurel and Hardy in their new feature length comedy, "Sons of the Desert," coming soon to the . . . . Theatre. "He's known as 'Goodtime Charley' and he is easily recognized by his peculiar characteristics and mannerisms. He is the fellow who slaps you so hard on the back that your false teeth are jarred loose. He slips up behind you and slips ice down your neck. His voice is the loudest—his clothes, likewise. His practical joking includes a varied line of tricks, the most popular number being the one where he pulls the chair from under you just as you are about to sit down. That's me to a tee in 'Sons of the Desert,'" declares Chase, with enthusiasm.

Members of Hollywood's famous American Legion Post, numbering more than one hundred, appear in atmospheric roles in "Sons of the Desert," Laurel and Hardy's new full-length feature comedy, to be shown soon at the . . . . Theatre. Included in the group are a drum and bugle corps, chanters and a drill team. The Santa Monica, California, Lodge of Elks is also represented in the picture in parade scenes which were photographed during a state convention of the antlered herd in the bay city a few months ago. During the actual filming of "Sons of the Desert," more than one thousand extra people were given employment as members of the supporting cast, which features Charley Chase, Mae Busch, Dorothy Christy and Lucien Littlefield.

•

Erring husbands who have been in the habit of using attendance at a national convention as an excuse for their dereliction, had better begin a subtle propaganda to keep their wives from viewing Laurel and Hardy's new full-length feature, "Sons of the Desert," to be shown soon at the . . . . Theatre. For "the lid will be off" once the comedy is thrown on the screen and the "inside" of many such gatherings exposed to the gaze of irate wives. "Sons of the Desert," declared by those who have previewed the picture to be one of the most hilarious comedies ever conceived, brings Laurel and Hardy to the screen as a couple of zealous fraternal brothers who pledge themselves to attend a convention of their order despite their wives' objections.

BELIEVE IT OR NOT—STAN LAUREL IS ONE COMIC WHO DOESN'T WANT TO DO HAMLET

Stan Laurel is one stellar screen comedian who would rather act the clown than do anything else his profession could offer. Hamlet or similar heavy roles do not appeal to him.

"You know this business of being funny is a lot of fun," Laurel will tell you when approached on the subject. "I get a great kick out of it. Many times I'll start some piece of comedy business and the sheer buffoonery of it will strike me so hard that I'll have all I can do to keep from laughing at my own antics. In fact, sometimes I'm unable to withhold a chuckle, and that generally means a re-take."

Laurel and Oliver Hardy, the other member of the internationally-known comedy team, star in "Sons of the Desert," the Hal Roach-M-G-M feature-length production opening . . . . at the . . . . Theatre.

Writes Own Stories

In addition to being a top-hole comedian, Laurel also writes a considerable portion of the stories he appears in. He has the almost perfect comedy sense and is capable of taking almost any given situation and turning it into sheer burlesque or low comedy. He is hardly the one to "dish out" subtle humor, although perfectly capable of doing so if necessary.

Often while appearing before the camera, he will get an inspiration, a certain gag or piece of business, which, although not appropriate for the film he is working in, could be used in some future production. As soon as the scene he is a part of is completed, he jots the idea down on a pad of paper that is always on hand for just this purpose. At home he elaborates on the idea and then places it in a filing cabinet which contains numerous similar material, all tabulated so that they might be of instant use whenever needed.

ONE WAY TO GET BETTER RESULTS

To save time and money, most scenes that take place in the same locale are "shot" at the same time in modern motion picture making. But Laurel and Hardy, starring in the Hal Roach-M-G-M feature-length comedy, "Sons of the Desert," coming to the . . . . Theatre, starting next . . . ., refuse to follow this procedure.

Arguing that their comedy depends considerably on spontaneity and that they find it frequently necessary to change various situations and gags in the script as they progress, this team of funsters insist on producing their film from continuity. That is, they make each scene in chronological order.

Naturally this is a far more costly process than that generally followed in the industry. It means many additional shifts of lights, sound equipment and other paraphernalia; also the carrying of people, until the entire film is completed, who otherwise would be discharged as soon as the various scenes they were registered in had been shot.

Wardrobe Never A Problem for Laurel & Hardy

Whether or not the adage concerning clothes making the man has any basis in fact, it is recognized within the ranks of the acting profession that garments go a long way toward establishing a character.

Many of the foremost comics of both the stage and screen are easily identified by the clothes they wear. Chaplin's baggy trousers and exaggerated shoes; Harold Lloyd's neat and perfect fitting suits; Buster Keaton's pancake hat; W. C. Field's frock coat, flashy waistcoat and high hat; and Laurel and Hardy's disreputable business suits and undersized derbies—all have contributed to the outstanding characterizations of the screen since its inception.

Genteel Shabbiness

In "Sons of the Desert," the Laurel and Hardy feature-length comedy opening . . . . at the . . . . Theatre, the funsters have no wardrobe problem. Their attire is that which has trade-marked them throughout the many years of their professional partnership. Genteel shabbiness seems to fit their screen personalities as no other raiment has, and but once in the past several years have the funsters discarded their stock habiliment in favor of more fetching attire. In "The Devil's Brother," their preceding full-length feature comedy, Stan and Oliver, appearing as roistering bandits, were clothed in appropriate period costumes.

Paradoxical as it may seem, the ill-fitting, seemingly cheap suits worn by Laurel and Hardy are the handiwork of high-priced tailors. Both their coats and trousers are fashioned out of expensive material and are carefully patterned to exaggerated dimensions. Cheap cloth will not stand up under the rough treatment the boys' clothes are subjected to and in order to attain the correct degree of bagginess and tightness essential to their respective suits, the comedians are carefully measured for their fittings.

Ten Suits a Year

At the beginning of each year, Laurel and Hardy place an order with their tailor for ten suits each, and if they are fortunate and don't play too rough, this wardrobe will carry them through the twelve-month period. Each of the suits costs sixty dollars. In some of their pictures, the funsters will wear out two or three suits or otherwise ruin them for future use.

Oliver Hardy, Charley Chase and Stan Laurel in "Sons of the Desert"

Cut or Mat 608-I

Cobweb on Set So Natural, It Fooled Spiders

When a technical department of a modern motion picture studio is requested to fill an attic set with cobwebs, it is handled in a routine manner. There was a time, however, when such an order would panic the most efficient property man and throw the various mechanical departments of a studio into confusion.

In the new Laurel and Hardy feature-length comedy, "Sons of the Desert," opening . . . . at the . . . . Theatre, one of the most humorous sequences in the picture transpires in a sadly-neglected attic. To carry out the illusion of its disuse, it was essential that cobwebs should hang from the eaves and rafters. Thirty minutes after this request was made, it was fulfilled.

Powder Spray Used

With the aid of a specially devised power spray gun, which operates on the same principle as the candy floss machines one sees at fairs and carnivals, dozens of simulated cobwebs — sufficiently realistic to intrigue the most wary spider — transfigured the newly-constructed garret with the desired effect. A mixture of glue and white lead with one other secret ingredient, shot through the power spray and diffused by means of centrifugal force, was all that was necessary to create the webs, which, in the "good old days" of the movies, would have cost a large sum of money as well as much effort.

A few days after Laurel and Hardy completed work in the attic sequence, one of the workmen on the stage where the set was still standing noticed that several of the large webs which had been broken during the filming had been completely repaired. Curious, he investigated further, and—believe it or not—he found two dead spiders in one of the artificial networks, indicating that the reconstruction work had been carried on by these valiant if gullible Arachnida.

They're Not Hawaiians but They Sure Know Their Hula-Hula!

The most graceful hula dancers are not always native Hawaiians.

At least this is the opinion of Dave Bennett, noted dance director for the stage and screen, who trained the line of "grass skirt wigglers" for the new Laurel and Hardy feature-length comedy, "Sons of the Desert," which starts a . . . . days' engagement at the . . . Theatre . . . .

The leader of the ensemble is 'Charita," a Spanish-Danish girl who was born in China. Other of the dancers are of Hawaiian-Korean and Hawaiian-Japanese descent. None of the girls was born in the islands.

The group was selected from more than five hundred applicants and represents the cream of the hula dancing talent in and around Los Angeles. In the Hal Roach-M-G-M feature comedy production, the girls present a novelty hula dance originated by Bennett.

Elected "Good Knight"

During the filming of Laurel and Hardy's new feature-length comedy, "Sons of the Desert," which comes to the . . . . Theatre next . . . ., members of the cast and the technicians organized a fraternal lodge of their own, taking for its name the title of the picture. Stan Laurel was elected "High Factotum," while Ollie Hardy was voted "Good Knight." Director Bill Seiter was chosen "Sergeant Without Arms."

STAN LAUREL ~ OLIVER HARDY in "SONS OF THE DESERT"

Cut or Mat 608-J

Use Own Names in Film Roles

Few actors permit the use of their own names to be attached to the characters they portray on the screen. Notable exceptions to this general rule are Stan Laurel and Oliver Hardy, who are co-starred in the Hal Roach-M-G-M full-length comedy feature, "Sons of the Desert," now playing at the . . . . Theatre.

As a pair of wayward husbands who sneak away to a lodge convention, the two actors call each other by their real names and also address their screen wives as Mrs. Laurel and Mrs. Hardy.

"It makes our performance more natural and also lends a certain intimacy to the roles we portray," explains Laurel, who suggested the departure. "Further, this procedure insures against confusion of the characters."

Stan Laurel, himself, is largely responsible for the various gags in "Sons of the Desert." Co-author of the story which gives the Hal Roach-M-G-M funster team the greatest vehicle they have yet appeared in, Laurel poured into the script a wealth of comedy gags and funny situations which he has noted during his long career behind the footlights and on the screen.

 **CATCHLINES** 

You'll laugh until the sands of the desert grow cold!

It's not always fair weather when good fellows get together!

They knew all the high signs but their wives did too!

They made merry while their wives made the best of it!

They were big shots to their lodge brothers but a pain in the neck to their wives!

They followed the doctor's orders but it didn't take!

While the cats stayed at home the mice romped at a convention!

Hail! Hail! The gang was all there . . . but oh, the morning after!

Wherein lodge rituals and marriage rituals conflict!

Their lodge gave them fancy grips . . . their wives gave them the "works."

They trod the hot sands both at their lodge and at home!

They were the life of the party until they had to settle up!

They were dizzy delegates at a dizzier convention!

When the bank struck up they struck out!

They were great mixers when they had the ingredients!

They could dish it out and they had to take it!

They were the life of the convention but mourners at home!

Laurel and Hardy in "Sons of the Desert"

Laurel and Hardy in "Sons of the Desert"

Cut or Mat 608-G

A Side-Splitting Show!

If you are interested in the grief you will entail should you lie to the "little woman" in order to get away for your lodge's convention, see Laurel and Hardy's full-length comedy feature, "Sons of the Desert," currently showing at the . . . . Theatre.

It's a funny story and the comic pair make it even funnier. As the husbands who have to deceive their wives in order to attend the "Sons of the Desert" convention in a distant city, Laurel and Hardy keep their audience convulsed as comic situation after comic situation unfolds to their extreme discomfort in each case.

Stanley's cry-baby tactics and Hardy's disgust at his mate's dumbness have never been better portrayed than in this exceedingly riotous comedy. It will keep the entire family roaring.

Hardy's meeting with his practical-joking brother-in-law, effectively and humorously played by Charley Chase, a star in his own right, creates laugh-provoking situations that add considerable life to the film.

Mae Busch, as Hardy's hard-boiled wife, and Dorothy Christy, as the beautiful, if nagging, spouse of Stanley's, prove perfect foils for the buffoonery of this inimitable duo of comics.

Golfer and Epicure

Amateur golfer, well-dressed man, and epicure! It is by these titles that Oliver Hardy is known in Hollywood. Although he weighs something over 250 pounds, he is one of the best amateur golfers in the movie colony. He has won more than thirty-five trophies for his prowess on the links. An epicure, Hardy will travel miles out of his way to sample some new dish he may have heard about, and he is no mean cook himself. He is a fastidious dresser and boasts one of the largest and most swagger wardrobes in all Hollywood.

Street, Night Club, Roof-Top All Within Stone's Throw Of Hal Roach Film Studio

It is no longer necessary to travel any great distance from a motion picture studio to obtain locations foreign to the locale where the studio is situated. With every department of the film industry organized to the highest possible degree, any scene imaginable can be photographed right on the company's own home "lot."

For instance, in the latest Laurel and Hardy feature-length comedy, "Sons of the Desert," which opens . . . . at the . . . . Theatre, the script called for locations in far separated portions of the country.

One was a Chicago street, another a Chicago night club, a third the roof of a Southern California residence, the interior of a Los Angeles duplex, a typical Los Angeles residential street and a large lodge meeting hall.

Not so many years ago, a call of this sort would have undoubtedly meant considerable extra financial expenditure for transportation of casts, technical staffs and equipment. However, with increased efficiency and equipment, the Hal Roach studio was enabled to fill every requirement of the film, "Sons of the Desert," right on its home lot at Culver City, California, which covers an area of 10 acres.

In fact, all the studio officials found missing was a Chicago street scene. This was constructed at a cost of $25,000, a comparatively small item when compared with what the expenditure would have been had the cast, staff and equipment been transported from Culver City to Chicago, where the scene was supposed to take place.

1,000 Extras Used

On this street, 1,000 extras waving banners and attired in fezzes and other convention apparel paraded to the tunes of typical lodge bands.

With this scene completed, it was a simple thing to shift all equipment a few blocks away to a sound stage, where a Chicago night club, complete in every detail, had been constructed.

The same was also true of every other scene called for by the script. Sound stages and other sets contained the necessary locations. In fact it was not found necessary to move out of the studio to shoot the California residential street scene. A realistic California street of homes was already part of the enormous studio equipment. All that was needed were a few minor changes to the street already on hand.

Thus, with the highest type of efficiency possible, the motion picture industry is able to shorten thousands of miles into so compact an area that it can be contained in a comparatively few acres of ground.

Director, Stumped on Convention Procedure, Makes Personal Investigation of Delegates

How do men act when they attend a lodge convention, especially if it is held a long distance from home and far away from the ever-watchful "little woman"?

This was one question that stumped Director William Seiter in megaphoning Laurel and Hardy's latest feature-length Hal Roach-M-G-M comedy, "Sons of the Desert," currently playing at the . . . . Theatre.

Of course many of those working on the lot, grips, electricians, cameramen and members of the cast had attended conventions of some sort or another at different times in their lives, but all of them had been so busy enjoying themselves that they hadn't paid much attention to the activities of others. However, as "Sons of the Desert" concerns itself considerably with a convention and some of the funniest sequences of the picture take place in the convention city, it was important that an authentic idea of just how things are carried on at such a gathering should be obtained.

A conference of everyone working on the film was called. All of those who had ever attended a convention, no matter how small or how large, were asked to give suggestions and a description of their experiences and the experiences of others they might know about. The result was a comparatively authentic idea of just what takes place in a convention city and among the conveners.

Not satisfied, however, Director Seiter and Laurel and Hardy made a trip to a nearby city where a large lodge convention was actually being held. After a few days of close observation, during which they mingled with the various delegations and talked with out-of-town members of the lodge, the trio came back to Hollywood fully prepared to truly portray the pleasurable activities of a lodge gathering in a strange city.

Their Wives "Dish It Out" and Laurel and Hardy "Take It"

They could dish it out and they had to take it! Paraphrasing the slang expression given wide currency recently, this summarizes the story of "Sons of the Desert," the Laurel and Hardy feature-length comedy now being shown at the . . . . Theatre.

As demonstrated by the two boys, the "dishing out" practice consists of deceiving their wives, who in turn are responsible for the ardent members of the "Sons of the Desert" lodge "taking it."

In order to attend a convention of their organization, Stan and Ollie are forced to resort to subterfuge. Skillfully, they devise a plot and with equal deftness win their wives' belief in their canny plans. All goes well until their deception is discovered, and then the fun begins!

COMIC FALLS BRING OLIVER HARDY MANY BRUISES—BUT IT'S ALL FOR ART'S SAKE!

"It must be a lot of fun and an easy way of making a living!" Hundreds of times both Stan Laurel and Babe Hardy have agreed to this assertion made by visitors to the Hal Roach studio who watch the two comics go through a scene or two of a current picture.

"It's much easier to agree with them than to start a debate," is the philosophical explanation of Oliver Hardy. "Furthermore, our 'fans' would be disillusioned if they thought that our work wasn't a continuous round of fun—not that we don't enjoy it and have a lot of laughs ourselves while making a picture.

"But there's another side to the story," continued Ollie. "For example, in our latest Hal Roach-M-G-M full-length feature, 'Sons of the Desert,' here are a few of the indignities and hardships we had to suffer while putting some real 'belly laughs' into the picture:

"I had to sit with my feet in a tub of boiling water for several minutes.

"I am crowned with a galvanized wash tub during an intimate scene with my screen wife.

"We were socked (and I mean SOCKED) on the fleshy portion of the anatomy with heavy slapsticks in the night club scene.

"Stan has to bump his head several times on the rafters in the attic sequence.

"We had to sit for hours one night on a roof-top with water pouring over us.

"I could go on and on enumerating the various and sundry abuses to which we are called upon to submit 'for the sake of our art' and if anyone thinks that this is fun, they should try working in comedies."

All in Day's Work

Despite the rotund star's protestations, it is apparent that both he and Stan Laurel consider the knocks and bumps they receive a part of the day's work and it is seldom that they balk at doing any stunt if it is good for a laugh.

Often, upon the completion of one of their pictures, either one or both of the comedians are a mass of black and blue spots, to say nothing of minor lacerations and scratches. They ruin several suits of clothes in their work during the course of the year.

In "Sons of the Desert," which comes to the . . . . Theatre next . . . ., Laurel and Hardy are seen in what is declared to be one of their most hilarious comedy features of recent years. In the supporting cast are Charley Chase, Mae Busch, Dorothy Christy, Lucien Littlefield and others.

Latest Laurel-Hardy Comedy A Grand Treat

When two wife-bedeviled husbands, Laurel and Hardy, find that they must attend their lodge's convention in Chicago, despite the strenuous objection of Hardy's wife, the latter invents a fictitious illness. With the assistance of a friendly horse doctor, who poses as an ethical physician, a trip to Hawaii is prescribed as a sure cure with the pair leaving for Chicago instead.

The resultant story-telling brings about a series of embarrassing situations, which with the assistance of Laurel and Hardy and Charley Chase, as the latter's brother-in-law, becomes a mirth-provoking film that should make "Sons of the Desert" the comedy hit of the year.

Hits New Comedy High

Now playing at the . . . . Theatre the production brings out the best in that outstanding team of funsters, Laurel and Hardy. Their escapades in the convention city and their return home turns the film into a comedy that even in these times hits a pre-depression high.

With the assistance of Charley Chase, who proves an unbeknown brother-in-law of Hardy's, the latter and Laurel help enliven the convention even though it causes them, in several incidents, near tragedy.

Their return home and the expose of their prevarications by "friend wives," Mae Busch and Dorothy Christy, are climaxes to a story that carries out the best traditions of this outstanding comedy pair. Among others in the cast is Lucien Littlefield, who essays the role of the veterinary.

Directed by William Seiter and produced by Hal Roach-M-G-M, it's the sort of picture you can't afford to miss if you enjoy a good hearty laugh.

Charley Chase Adds Guffaws To Fun Frolic

For the first time in his career since he attained stardom, Charley Chase, popular Hal Roach comedian, is appearing in the cast of a picture other than his own.

Reading the script of "Sons of the Desert," the new Laurel and Hardy full length feature comedy, one day recently, Chase was intrigued by a "good time Charlie" part in the story and he immediately sought out Director William Seiter and suggested that he be given the role.

When Seiter recovered from the shock of a star offering to appear in support of others, he immediately secured Charley's signature on the dotted line of a contract and then asked the actor to explain himself.

"Why, there's no catch to it," explained Chase. "I'm delighted at the opportunity to work with Stan and Oliver and the part, as I see it, is made to order for me."

Chase, who has a large fan following of his own, has been a Hal Roach-M-G-M stellar comedian for many years and has appeared in scores of fun films under this banner. He and Laurel and Hardy have been warm friends since they first met on the Roach "lot" and each is an admirer of the other's peculiar comedy talents. There has never been any professional jealousy among the three funsters and on many occasions they have exchanged ideas for their respective comedy offerings.

"Sons of the Desert," which begins a . . . . days' engagement at the . . . . Theatre next . . . ., boasts of an eminent supporting cast, including, besides Chase, such well known players as Mae Busch, Dorothy Christy and Lucien Littlefield.

TRIPLE LAUGHS

Cut or Mat 608-L

When three such rousing comics as Stan Laurel, Oliver Hardy and Charley Chase get together you can expect an entertainment of riotous proportions. As a trio of timid souls who attempt to forget their matrimonial troubles at a fraternal convention, "Sons of the Desert" gives them every opportunity for their inimitable laugh talents. The picture is currently playing at the . . . . Theatre.

A PREVIEW RAVE!

—there'll be scores more like these!

(Reprinted from "The Hollywood Reporter," November 10, 1933)

NEW LAUREL AND HARDY FEATURE IS GOOD FUN

Story Different and Direction Top Notch

"SONS OF THE DESERT"

(Hal Roach-MGM)

Director_____William A. Seiter

Author ________Byron Morgan

Photographer____Kenneth Peach

Cast: Oliver Hardy, Stan Laurel, Charley Chase, Mae Busch, Dorothy Christy and Lucien Littlefield.

The new Laurel and Hardy comedy, "Sons of the Desert," has nothing at all to do with the desert, but plenty to do with real genuine laughter.

This picture is as good as any of the Laurel and Hardy comedies. It's new slap-stick and not at all hard to take.

The team is especially fortunate in its supporting cast. Mae Busch does herself proud as Hardy's wife, and Dorothy Christy is a good match for her as Laurel's spouse. Lucien Littlefield has a small but telling part, and Charley Chase adds some comedy all his own.

Laurel and Hardy are members of a lodge called "The Sons of the Desert," the oaths containing a solemn not-to-be-broken pledge to attend the annual convention in Chicago. Both the men being henpecked husbands, the getting-away presents difficulties. Hardy, however, overcomes them by developing a tremendous nervous breakdown and being ordered to Honolulu by a doctor who has been bribed.

So, off to the convention they go, and have a high old time, returning home to their wives all unaware that the boat on which they are supposed to be returning from Honolulu has been sunk, and the rescue ship is due the day after their arrival.

Laurel and Hardy are grand in this film. Laurel is not so completely and continuously squelched, and the two seem to work together even more deftly than usual. William A. Seiter's direction was pointed for comedy, Kenneth Peach's photography is good, and Byron Morgan's story is different.

Don't worry about this picture wherever Laurel and Hardy are liked. It is good, adequate, dependable comedy.

LAUREL and HARDY MASKS

PLACE THEM ON YOUR OUTSIDE BOX-OFFICE, SIDES OF THEATRE, OVER ORCHESTRA ENTRANCE, AS A SPECIAL DISPLAY ON LOBBY EASEL OR WALL OR IN ANY ARRANGEMENT BEST SUITED TO YOUR HOUSE.

MEASUREMENTS. Each mask is 31 inches high, 20 inches wide, 9 inches deep.

Designed and modeled by the famous modern sculptor, Willi Noell. Painted in natural poster colors with satin waterproof finish.

Shipped by express, C.O.D.—charges collect.

PRICE PER SET

(2 masks)—$10.00 net, includes packing

WRITE OR WIRE YOUR ORDER DIRECT TO

R. FIORE

72 THOMAS STREET, NEW YORK CITY, N. Y.

A PREVIEW RAVE!

—there'll be scores more like these!

(Reprinted from "The Hollywood Reporter," November 10, 1933)

NEW LAUREL AND HARDY FEATURE IS GOOD FUN

Story Different and Direction Top Notch

"SONS OF THE DESERT"
(Hal Roach-MGM)

Director______William A. Seiter

Author ________Byron Morgan

Photographer____Kenneth Peach

Cast: Oliver Hardy, Stan Laurel, Charley Chase, Mae Busch, Dorothy Christy and Lucien Littlefield.

The new Laurel and Hardy comedy, "Sons of the Desert," has nothing at all to do with the desert, but plenty to do with real genuine laughter.

This picture is as good as any of the Laurel and Hardy comedies. It's new slap-stick and not at all hard to take.

The team is especially fortunate in its supporting cast. Mae Busch does herself proud as Hardy's wife, and Dorothy Christy is a good match for her as Laurel's spouse. Lucien Littlefield has a small but telling part, and Charley Chase adds some comedy all his own.

Laurel and Hardy are members of a lodge called "The Sons of the Desert," the oaths containing a solemn not-to-be-broken pledge to attend the annual convention in Chicago. Both the men being henpecked husbands, the getting-away presents difficulties. Hardy, however, overcomes them by developing a tremendous nervous breakdown and being ordered to Honolulu by a doctor who has been bribed.

So, off to the convention they go, and have a high old time, returning home to their wives all unaware that the boat on which they are supposed to be returning from Honolulu has been sunk, and the rescue ship is due the day after their arrival.

Laurel and Hardy are grand in this film. Laurel is not so completely and continuously squelched, and the two seem to work together even more deftly than usual. William A. Seiter's direction was pointed for comedy, Kenneth Peach's photography is good, and Byron Morgan's story is different.

Don't worry about this picture wherever Laurel and Hardy are liked. It is good, adequate, dependable comedy.

LAUREL and HARDY MASKS

PLACE THEM ON YOUR OUTSIDE BOX-OFFICE, SIDES OF THEATRE, OVER ORCHESTRA ENTRANCE, AS A SPECIAL DISPLAY ON LOBBY EASEL OR WALL OR IN ANY ARRANGEMENT BEST SUITED TO YOUR HOUSE.

MEASUREMENTS. Each mask is 31 inches high, 20 inches wide, 9 inches deep.

Designed and modeled by the famous modern sculptor, Willi Noell. Painted in natural poster colors with satin waterproof finish.

Shipped by express, C.O.D.—charges collect.

PRICE PER SET

(2 masks)—$10.00 net, includes packing

WRITE OR WIRE YOUR ORDER DIRECT TO

R. FIORE

72 THOMAS STREET, NEW YORK CITY, N. Y.

TIMELY ADVICE TO DRINKERS — *How NOT to Open a Bottle!*

10" Cut or Mat No. 608-EC

BY THOSE INVENTIVE COMICS—LAUREL AND HARDY—IN THEIR FULL-LENGTH FEATURE COMEDY—"SONS OF THE DESERT"

There is a ceremonious technique to the opening of a champagne bottle and for the benefit of Repealists, Laurel and Hardy have revived this ancient ritual. Here's how!

OLLIE: "This is a fine mess. Here's a bottle of rare old vintage but we haven't a bottle opener."

STAN: "I have a bottle opener, Ollie, but it's at home. But wait, here's a swell idea . . ."

OLLIE: "That's no way to open an expensive bottle of champagne. Do you want to ruin your new bridgework? Here, let me have it; I'll show you!"

STAN: "There's (hic!) nobody who knows more about this than I do. The guy that corked this must have used a sledge hammer . . . it can't be done!"

OLLIE: "That gives me an idea; ask the waiter if he has a small hammer. When good fellows get together they MUST have a drink!"

STAN: "I'll sock it gently—you hold the bottle steady. Here it goes!"

OLLIE: "See, Stan, it's all in knowing how!"

BOTH: "Here's Happy Days, you old Son of the Desert."

Stan Laurel, Oliver Hardy and Charley Chase will appear in their convulsing burlesque of a fraternal order, "Sons of the Desert," wherein the audience is introduced to secret high signs, distress signals and a hilarious convention of delegates. This Metro-Goldwyn-Mayer full-length picture will be shown at Loew's State Theatre on December 29th, 30th and 31st.

LIQUOR IS FRONT PAGE NEWS

Liquor repeal and its many aftermaths is front page news in all wet states. Repeal is still so new after their years of prohibition that people are getting a kick out of everything pertaining to their alcoholic freedom. Play dates around New Year have a double chance of planting above halftone strip or using it as bottle wraparound by stores or places licensed to sell wet goods.

HERE'S PLENTY OF EXTRA PROMOTION

ORDER 10 INCH CUT OR MAT NO. 608-EA

WHEN GOOD FELLOWS GET TOGETHER — *How to Recognize a Fraternal Brother!*

THE GRIP. When you think you have spotted a fellow member in public, raise your right hand with thumb extended. If he does the same instantly and immediately interlocks his fingers with yours without fumbling, you'll know you have met a worthy brother of that great fraternal order, "Sons of the Desert."

THE HIGH SIGN. Should the stranger fail to respond, test him with the High Sign. This consists of extending the fingers of your right hand towards him, resting elbow on the closed left fist. This is one of the most closely guarded secrets of our ritual and only bona-fide members can do it expertly.

THE DISTRESS SIGNAL. Oliver Hardy is not recoursing to deaf and dumb language, but is trying to secure the attention of his fellow lodge member, Stan Laurel, who fears a "touch" and pretends preoccupation. Any fellow member who ignores the Distress Signal of a duly qualified brother faces immediate expulsion.

BROTHER CAN YOU SPARE A DIME? Always keep your money planted somewhere else in your suit so that when impecunious or brothers in the red ask you the foregoing question you can instantly turn out your trouser pockets as evidence of being in the same situation. It never fails to work and is one of the most effective signs in our ritual.

As Exemplified by STAN LAUREL *and* OLIVER HARDY *in "Sons of the Desert"*

Stan Laurel, Oliver Hardy Hardy and Charley Chase attend the convention of their secret lodge, "Sons of the Desert," and when these good fellows get together in their annual whoopee high signs are mixed, distress signals ignored and initiations give audiences laugh hysterics. "Sons of the Desert" is their latest full-length feature picture for Metro-Goldwyn-Mayer and will be shown at Loew's State Theatre for three days, beginning Friday, December 29th.

3-DAY CONTEST

Cut or Mat Series No. 608-EB

Screen comics—those well and favorably known—are always excellent subjects of this kind and when accompanying publicity articles explain that the filled in faces should show the expressions characteristic of a rough and rowdy initiation into a secret lodge, the imagination of the reader immediately suggests that "Sons of the Desert" ought to be an extremely funny full-length comedy.

SOCKO! Oliver Hardy Is Initiated! Draw His Expression for Tickets

AWARDS OF 50 GUEST TICKETS GIVEN FOR BEST FILLED IN FACES. RIGHT EXPRESSIONS ARE IMPORTANT.

Oliver Hardy was just given the "works" while being initiated into that convulsing fraternal order, "Sons of the Desert," Metro-Goldwyn-Mayer's latest full-length comedy picture.

You've seen him dozens of times in previous short comedies with his inseparable partner, Stan Laurel, and know what his face looks like.

Make your mental image of his face conform with the expression you think he should show while he is being initiated—fear, surprise, amusement, indignation, etc.

Two more similar sketches of Stan Laurel and Charley Chase will appear in the Daily Star during the next two days.

All you have to do is fill in the missing faces, according to instructions, and submit the drawings to "Sons of the Desert" Editor before Wednesday, December 27th. For the most appropriate expressions there will be ticket awards of two pairs each to 50 persons.

Anything—ink, watercolors or pencil may be used. Save this sketch until all three outlines are filled in and then mail them. Watch for tomorrow's reproduction.

"Sons of the Desert" satirizes lodge and fraternal orders with broad hilarious comedy. Oliver Hardy, Stan Laurel and Charley Chase are the stars and this full-length feature will be shown at Loew's State Theatre on December 29th, 30th and 31st.

Lodge Brothers Give Stan Laurel the Works! Guest Tickets

HE'LL NEVER FORGET IT! AND NEITHER WILL YOU—FOR TICKETS AND LAUGHS! DRAW IN HIS EXPRESSION.

Here is the second sketch in the series of three, last one appearing in tomorrow's Daily Star.

You supply the missing features but first you must remember that Stan Laurel is in the process of being initiated into that hilarious secret fraternal order, "Sons of the Desert," which is also the title of Metro-Goldwyn-Mayer's newest full-length feature comedy picture.

The face of this celebrated comic is familiar to every movie fan, but in this instance you must show the expression which would be characteristic of the applicant's induction into the maddest of lodges—horror, fear, disbelief, surprise, anger, etc.

Oliver Hardy's sketch appeared yesterday and Charley Chase's will be shown tomorrow. When you have all three filled in, according to daily instructions, mail them to the "Sons of the Desert" Editor, on or before Wednesday, December 27th.

Try it with pencil, ink, crayon or watercolors. 50 pairs of Guest Tickets are the awards for the best sets of three filled-in outlines.

"Sons of the Desert" stars three great comics of the screen—Stan Laurel, Oliver Hardy and Charley Chase—in a full length comedy picture just packed with laughs. The guest tickets are for its showing at Loew's State Theatre on December 29th, 30th and 31st.

GAG IT IN PUBLIC VEHICLES

PASSING OUT CIRCULARS WITH FULL INFORMATION

LAUREL AND HARDY DOUBLES, OR ANY OTHER TWO MEN, TO TRAVEL ON ALL PUBLIC CONVEYANCES AND GAG THE PICTURE WITH FANTASTIC AND LUDICROUS FRATERNAL ORDER SIGNS AND GRIPS. THEY PASS OUT THEATRE LEAFLETS AT EACH CONCLUSION.

You've worked similar ideas before but with this feature-length comedy it's a natural for laughs and box-office impetus.

TRAILER

Write or wire for it to the

NATIONAL SCREEN SERVICE

Branch addresses are:

126 W. 46th St., New York City
810 South Wabash Ave., Chicago, Ill.
1922 South Vermont Ave., Los Angeles, Cal.
300½ South Harwood Ave., Dallas, Texas
141 Walton St., Atlanta, Ga.

Charley Chase Joins "Sons of the Desert." Last Chance for Tickets

LAST CHANCE FOR GUEST TICKET AWARDS AS DAILY STAR'S CONTEST CLOSES TODAY.

Here is the third and last outline face in the "Sons of the Desert" contest.

It's our old friend, Charley Chase, who together with Stan Laurel and Oliver Hardy make "Sons of the Desert" the funniest full-length comedy that Metro-Goldwyn-Mayer has ever made.

Charley is one of the trio receiving his initiation into this screamingly funny burlesque of secret societies and fraternal orders, "Sons of the Desert."

What expression you fill in is entirely a matter of personal opinion, but it is well to remember that a strenuous initiation generally leaves the applicant filled with rage, consternation, apprehension, fear, surprise, etc. One of these expressions is what you should strive to obtain when you draw in his features.

Mail this one of Charley Chase, together with those of Stan Laurel and Oliver Hardy of previous appearances, to "Sons of the Desert Editor" before noon tomorrow, December 27th.

For the best filled-in sets of three each artist-reader will receive a pair of Guest Tickets to Loew State Theatre's most hilarious and convulsing full-length comedy picture shown there in years. Dates of the "Sons of the Desert" engagement are December 29th, 30th and 31st.

THEY DON'T COST MUCH — 10" x 4"

THROWAWAY SLIPS AT INEXPENSIVE PRICES FOR LOCAL LODGE AND CLUB MAILING LISTS AND PASSING OUT IN ADVANCE TO THE GENERAL PUBLIC. PRINTED IN DARK GREEN ON SALMON COLORED PAPER.

PRICES (Including theatre name and play dates in copy): 1000—$3.00; 3000—$2.75 Per M; 5000—$2.50 Per M; 10,000—$2.25 Per M. Shipping charges extra. Order Direct from ECONOMY PRINTING CO., 239 West 39th Street, New York City.

DESERT
DESERT
SONS OF THE
DESERT
LOS ANGELES
OASIS 13
MG.34701

SASHES and FEZZES FOR ADVANCE PLUG

AN ADAPTATION OF THE SASH AND FEZ WORN BY LAUREL AND HARDY AND THE OTHER FRATERNAL DELEGATES IN THE PICTURE. PLACE THEM ON THEATRE PERSONNEL AT LEAST A WEEK IN ADVANCE OF PLAY DATES.

Order Direct from

MORRIS LIBERMAN
729 Broadway
New York City

Shipping Charges Extra

FEZ HATS. 35 cents each. Made of felt. Yellow design and lettering on maroon background. Tasseled. Supplied in one size only—which will fit the average head.

SASHES. Made of satin. Pins behind shoulder and under left arm. 25 cents each.

MOCK INITIATIONS

Properly sashed and placarded, a local initiation or snake dance of "The Sons of the Desert" ought to give the public many a laugh and strong inclination to see the picture. It can be done with high school or college students,

theatre personnel, members of a boys' club, unemployed men, etc. A few or many participants is optional with the theatre. Perform it through the city, in front of your theatre or on the stage in the form of an initiation ceremony.

OTHER MATERIAL FROM LIBERMAN

Theatres desiring special valance, flag or any other theatre accessory can procure it from the manufacturer, Morris Liberman, 729 Broadway, N. Y. C., by writing or wiring him direct. Selling or rental prices are the same as on any other material illustrated and described in previous M-G-M press books.

LOCAL LODGE NIGHTS THEATRE GUESTS

Shriners, Odd Fellows, Red Men, Knights of Columbus, Knights of Pythias, Foresters and all other secret fraternal orders should be invited as guests of the management, or at a greatly reduced price, on designated nights.

BANNERS MANUFACTURED TO ORDER—$2.75 EACH
SIZE 3x9 FEET. ORDER DIRECT FROM
MORRIS LIBERMAN
729 BROADWAY, NEW YORK CITY

Hang a banner under your marquee or in the lobby in honor of each invited lodge. This slapstick burlesque of fraternal orders—their rituals, initiations and conventions—will delight and afford great amusement to every member with a sense of humor—and nearly all of them have it.

Los Angles, Oasis 13, Sons of the Desert.

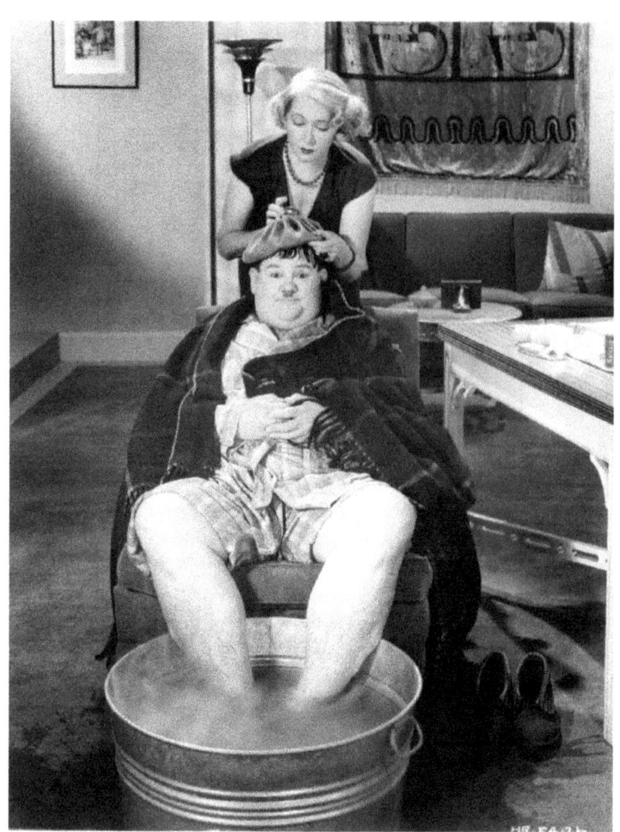

Oliver Hardy and Mae Busch.

Mae Busch, Dorothy Christie, Oliver Hardy, and Stan Laurel.

Charley Chase with one of the "Honolulu Babies".

Canvas Standard

28″ by 40″. Made of canvas with fringed bottom. $1.50 each with crossbar. $1.25 without crossbar.

ORDER DIRECT FROM

MORRIS LIBERMAN

729 BROADWAY, N. Y. C.

SHIPPING CHARGES EXTRA

6-FOOT

LOBBY DISPLAY

For the benefit of exhibitors who did not order this cutout, presented for the first time on the previous full-length Laurel and Hardy picture, "The Devil's Brother," we again reproduce it as a year round accessory.

Your sign painter simply changes billing to conform to your latest Laurel and Hardy full-length or short subject picture and you have an outside or inside theatre display in which initial cost is recouped many times with the extra admissions it will always bring.

Attractively hand-colored and it will advertise both "Coming" and "Now Playing" attractions.

$6.50 EACH IN BLACK AND WHITE

$9.50 EACH IN COLORS

ORDER DIRECT FROM National Studios, Inc., 226 West 56th St., N. Y. C. Shipping charges extra. Send remittance with order. Both prices include hinged easel-back.

GREAT CHANCE FOR A FLOAT

Use a small truck, placing striped awning material around sides, back and front, while the body should carry a heaping pile of sand and a few small palm trees.

Use the fez-hatted cutout 24-sheet heads of Laurel and Hardy, mounted back to back on compo board.

Same idea would make an excellent window display worked through a peep hole arrangement or without window covering.

Sand Envelopes

Placing sand in teaser envelope on "desert" pictures is a fairly popular exploitation stunt and with this title you have a chance to repeat.

Enclose appropriate theatre leaflet, prepared locally from any of the material in press book, and pass out several thousand of them.

DRESS THEATRE WITH FRATERNAL ORDER FLAGS AND INSIGNIA

"Sons of the Desert" is a very funny burlesque of an imaginary fraternal order. There is nothing mean or spiteful in it and nothing to which any intelligent group of officers of local lodges in your town can take exception.

Whether or not you intend holding special performances in honor of the various local orders, you should make every effort to dress up marquee and lobby with their flags and banners for the additional color and atmosphere it will give your theatre and the personal good will or flavor it will inject into your engagement.

We'd even hold a special screening for officers if it's necessary to secure the necessary cooperation.

PAPER FEZ HATS

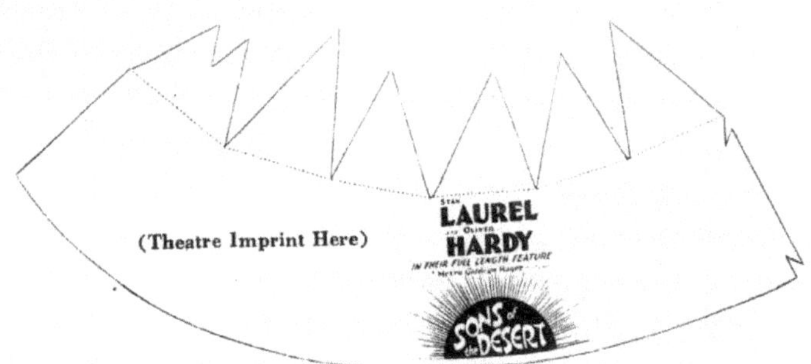

WHEN OPENED THIS PAPER FEZ HAT MEASURES ABOUT 22" BY 8". PRINTED ON STRONG YELLOW CARDBOARD. PAINTED-ON TASSEL APPEARS ON ONE SIDE. SLITTED TO MAKE CIRCULAR FOLDING QUICK AND EASY.

Showing how the Paper Fez Hat will look when actually worn.

THEATRES with very little dough will look with favor on this special and comparatively inexpensive cardboard accessory for mock initiations, street stunts, newsboys, boys' clubs and students invited to attend in groups at a special admission price and for wearing to theatres by various members of fraternal orders invited to be the guests of the management.

PRICES:

25—$2.00; 50—$3.00; 100—$4.00; 250—$7.50; 500—$12.50; 1,000—$20.00. Delivered flat, die-cut and ready to fold.

IMPRINTING THEATRE NAMES AND PLAY DATES ON THE SIDE: $1.00 extra regardless of quantity.

ORDER DIRECT FROM Economy Printing Co., 239 West 39th Street, New York City. Shipping charges extra.

LOCAL CONVENTION PICTURES FOR IDENTIFICATION

Each of your local fraternal orders has convention or annual get-together pictures in which most of the membership participated. It might be possible to obtain several of these from different lodges for guest ticket newspaper identification. Specify that each member presenting himself with a marked newspaper reproduction at the box-office must do so between certain hours in order to keep free admissions down. Another method is to work it in conjunction with your various fraternal order nights.

Sandpaper Faces

Heads or masks fashioned locally by theatres from sheets of sandpaper provide another method of street exploiting this attraction. Timely copy, tied up with "Sons of the Desert" title, will complete a startling and interesting stunt.

Ballyhoos like this have been done before by razor blade companies, and with "Desert" connoting sand, it should appeal to some theatres.

William A. Seiter, Oliver Hardy, Stan Laurel.

Staged still with Stan Laurel, Oliver Hardy, and Charley Chase.

START A "SONS OF THE DESERT" LODGE

THE most extensive club organization, for motion picture exploitation, was "Brothers Under the Skin" of 12 years ago. That was a stunt truly national in scope because every newspaper of importance in the country fell for it.

Since that time M-G-M has suggested similar formations for other picture promotion—its most recent being "Red Headed Woman."

You have another great opportunity with "Sons of the Desert," its story of a fraternal order of the same name providing an ideal subject.

Local formation of the "Sons of the Desert" is easily possible through the services of a friendly judge to whom you can present articles of incorporation prepared by you or lawyer-acquaintance. Strictest secrecy should be maintained about the picture title and no advance theatre publicity should be released until the gag has served its purpose.

The "founders" or "charter members," after the articles of incorporation are signed, hold an advertising meeting at some prominent place with the assistance of a knowing or unacquainted press. Plants are generously distributed throughout the first meeting to create dissension and you can "discover" in attendance some girl dressed in man's clothing. Anything to create excitement, together with plenty of human interest angles, are the things to work for in your meetings at which you must not forget to pass out Application Blanks and have photographers present.

This suggestion can be worked out in any fair-sized city and with the "breaks" it always gets plenty of big publicity spreads.

A LAUGH IN EVERY MEMBERSHIP

APPLICATION

SIZE 8¼ INCHES BY 7¼ INCHES

In some cases it will be possible to obtain use of membership lists of fraternal orders so that you can mail an application blank to each member.

Also distribute extra copies via theatre, street, mail, parked cars and slip under residence doors.

Size 8¼ in. by 7¼ in. Printed in red on yellow paper. Comparatively inexpensive novelty of which even the smallest theatre can afford a thousand.

PRICES (Including theatre imprint and play dates): 500—$3.00; 1000—$4.00; 3000—$3.75 Per M; 5000—$3.50 Per M; 10,000—$3.25 Per M.

Order direct from ECONOMY PRINTING CO., 239 West 39th Street, New York City. Shipping charges extra.

The "Sons" created for the theater publicity has no connection to the modern Sons of the Desert, now over 50 years old.

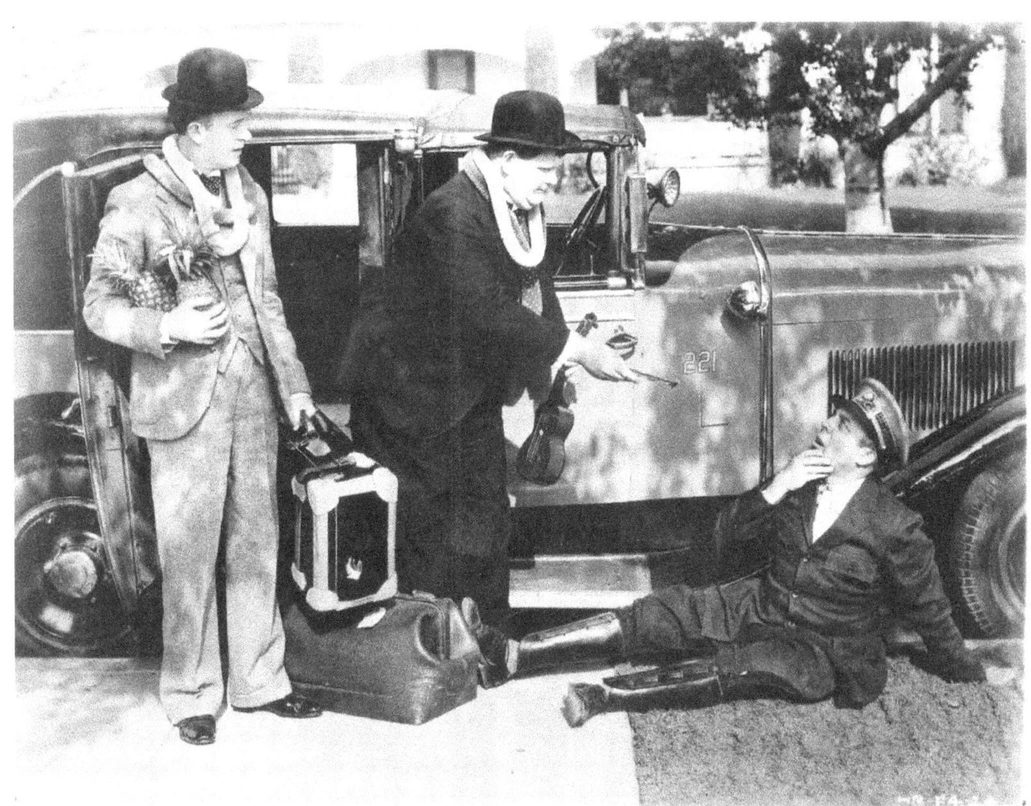

Laurel and Hardy arrive back home after the Honolulu trip that was never taken.

Fraternal brothers arrive home.

NEWSPAPER ADS

Three-Col. Ad Cut or Mat No. 608-A7

THEIR NEW FULL-LENGTH
FEATURE PICTURE!
Stan
LAUREL
Oliver
HARDY
in
'SONS OF
THE DESERT'
An
M-G-M
Picture

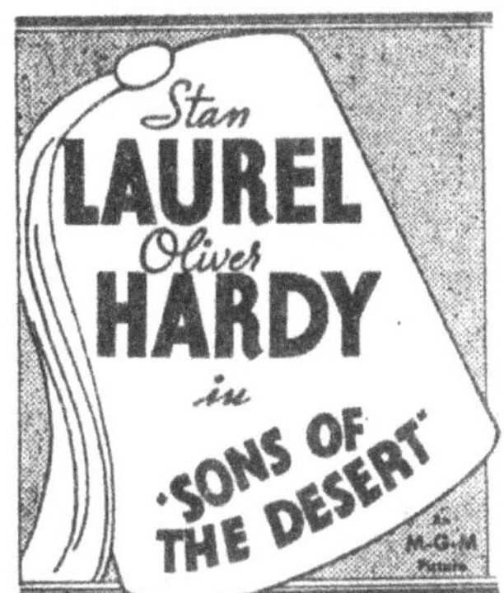

One-Col. Slug Cut or Mat No. 608-A2

THEIR NEW FULL-LENGTH
FEATURE PICTURE!
STAN
LAUREL
OLIVER
HARDY
in
SONS OF
THE DESERT
An
M-G-M
Picture

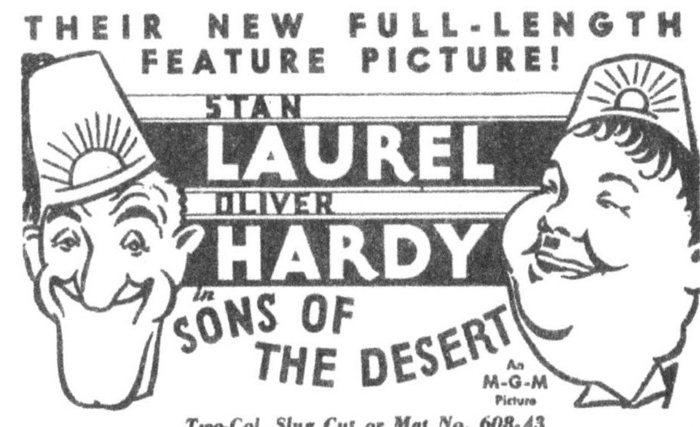

Two-Col. Slug Cut or Mat No. 608-A3

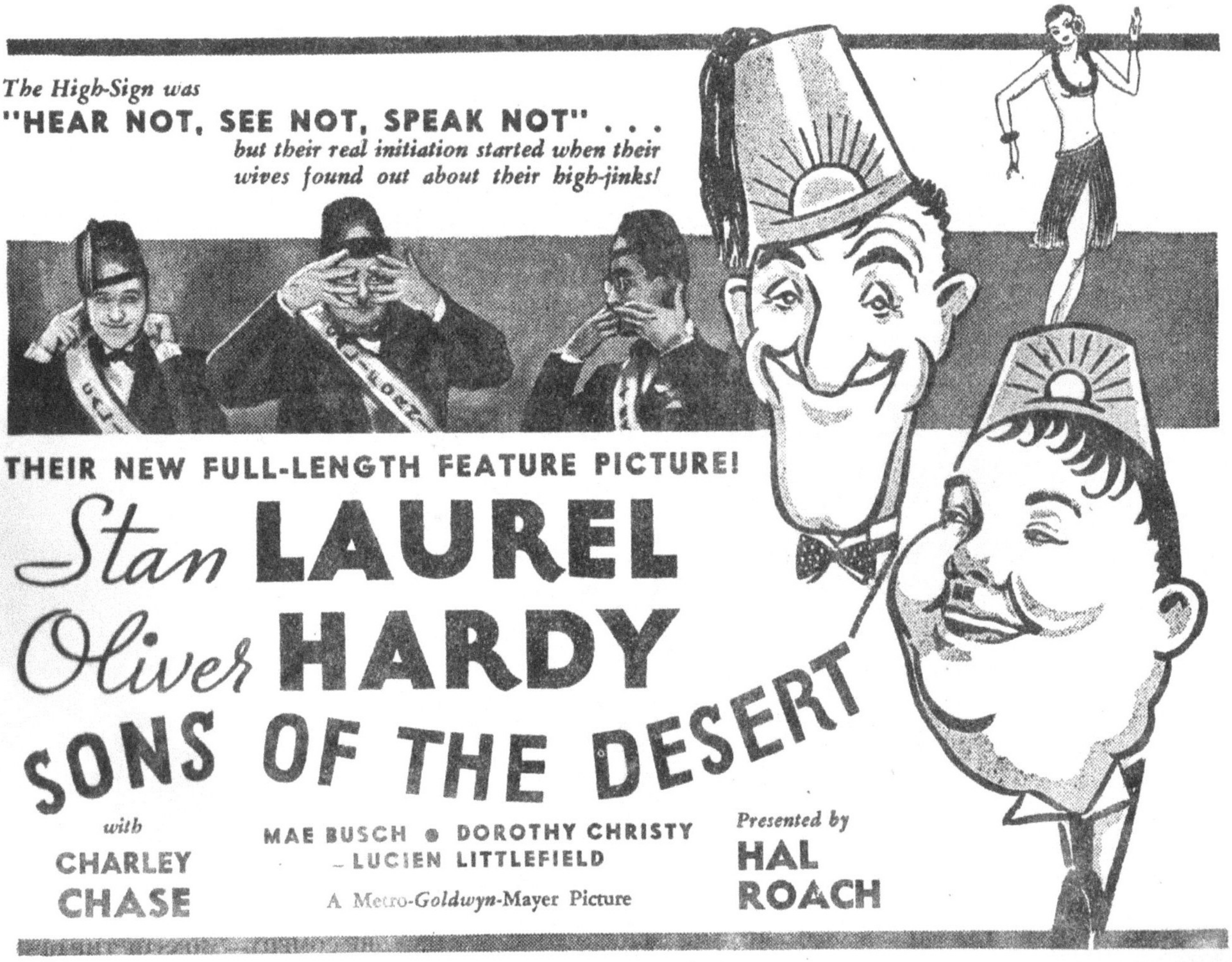
The High-Sign was
"HEAR NOT, SEE NOT, SPEAK NOT" . . .
but their real initiation started when their
wives found out about their high-jinks!
THEIR NEW FULL-LENGTH FEATURE PICTURE!
Stan LAUREL
Oliver HARDY
SONS OF THE DESERT
with
CHARLEY
CHASE
MAE BUSCH • DOROTHY CHRISTY
– LUCIEN LITTLEFIELD
A Metro-Goldwyn-Mayer Picture
Presented by
HAL
ROACH

Four-Col. Ad Cut or Mat No. 608-A1

Two-Col. Ad Cut or Mat No. 608-A14

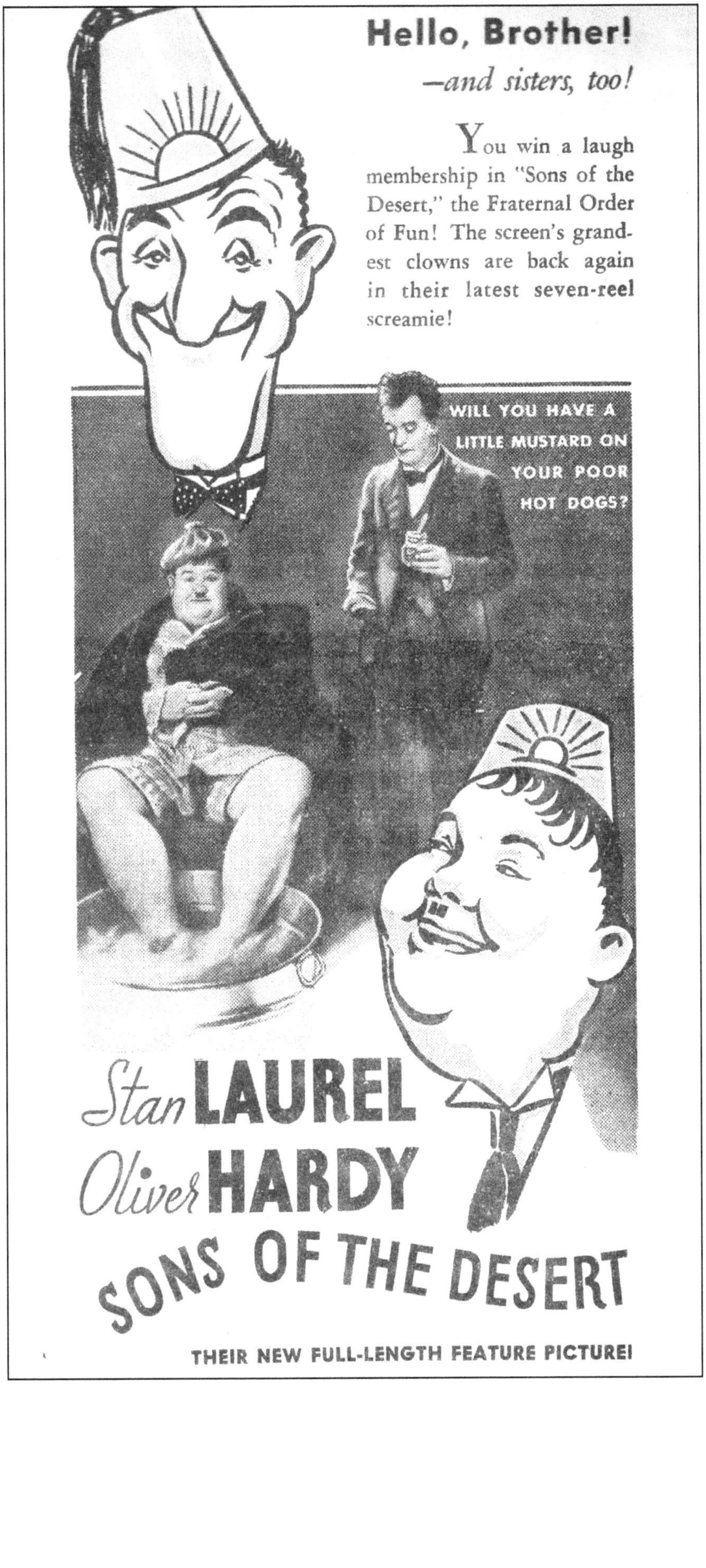

Hello, Brother!

—and sisters, too!

You win a laugh membership in "Sons of the Desert," the Fraternal Order of Fun! The screen's grandest clowns are back again in their latest seven-reel screamie!

WILL YOU HAVE A LITTLE MUSTARD ON YOUR POOR HOT DOGS?

Stan LAUREL
Oliver HARDY
SONS OF THE DESERT

THEIR NEW FULL-LENGTH FEATURE PICTURE!

THEIR NEW FULL- LENGTH FEATURE PICTURE!

One-Col. Slug Cut or Mat No. 608-A5

One-Col. Ad Cut or Mat No. 608-A4

Three-Col. Ad Cut or Mat No. 608-A13

Two-Col. Ad Cut or Mat No. 608-A10

Two-Col. Ad Cut or Mat No. 608-A9

One-Col. Slug Cut or Mat No. 608-A6

One-Col. Slug Cut or Mat No. 608-A12

YOU'LL LAUGH TILL IT HURTS!

Laurel and Hardy they went to a party,
It was their lodge convention;
They attracted the ladies by raising old Hades
And also attracted attention.

When they got home, they thought, all alone,
They'd sit down and start reminiscing;

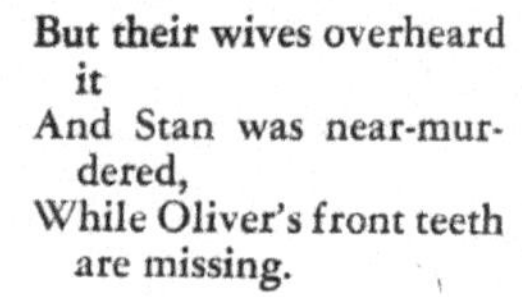
But their wives overheard it
And Stan was near-murdered,
While Oliver's front teeth are missing.

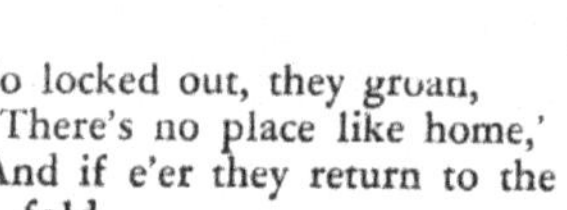
So locked out, they groan,
"There's no place like home,'
And if e'er they return to the fold,
They vow not to mention
That blamed old convention
Till the Sons of the Desert grow cold.

THEIR NEW FULL-LENGTH FEATURE PICTURE!

STAN LAUREL · OLIVER HARDY

in

"SONS of the DESERT"

(Theatre Name, Date and Small Billing)

with

CHARLEY CHASE

• MAE BUSCH •
DOROTHY CHRISTY
LUCIEN LITTLEFIELD

Directed by
WILLIAM A. SEITER

A Metro-Goldwyn-Mayer Picture

AD MAKE-OVERS

A greater variety of newspaper ads and ad sizes may be obtained by re-arranging the units of the ads illustrated on other pages of this book. Simply cut the mats apart as indicated below. Insert copy in the spaces provided.

3 COL. x 5"

3 COL. x 4½"

2 COL. x 2"

1 COL. x 8"

1 COL. X 5¼"

2 COL. X 11½"

Stan
LAUREL
Oliver
HARDY
SONS OF THE
DESERT

2 COL. X 7"

2 COL. X 5"

POSTER CUTOUTS

Actual canvas tent on marquee or lobby, or even a painted one, will add a lot of box-office appeal to the 24-sheet cutout. Mount heads on compo and arrange so that they fill opening.

Emphasize top phrase with a circle so that people will know immediately you are showing a full-length comedy and not a short. Rest of 3-sheet lends itself to a strong cut-out.

6 - sheet above secured simply by removing billing to the bottom.

1-sheet design which is ideal for shadow box display. The sun and its rays should be cut out for background illumination worked on a flasher.

Extreme right illustrates the second 3—also a simple cut out job obtained by notching side and between heads.

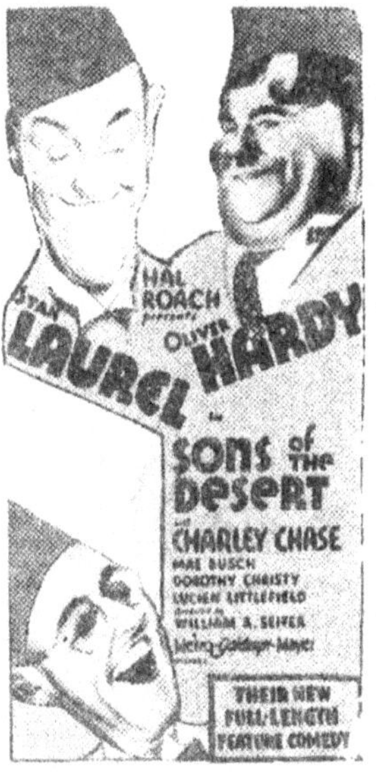

WINDOW CARD

HERALD

ONE SHEET (Style D)

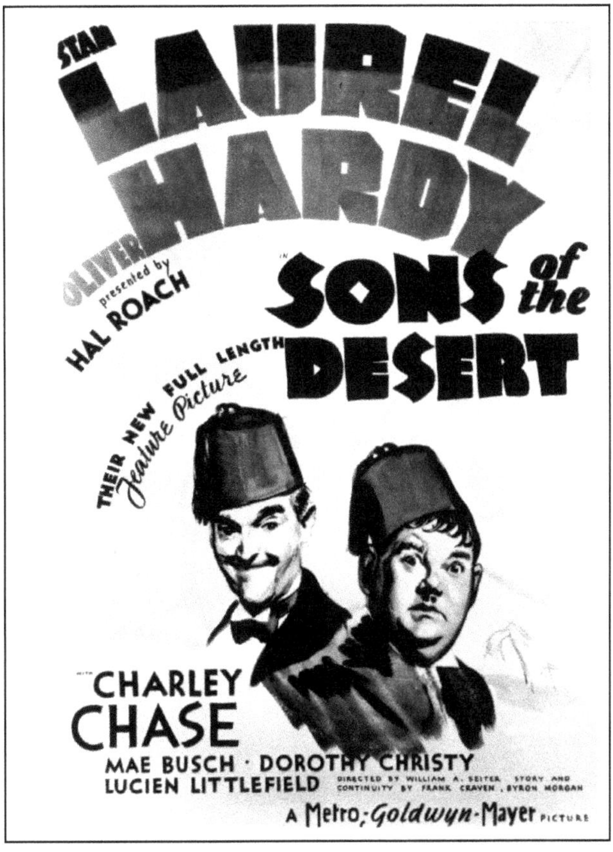

BILLBOARD (24 sheet)

LOBBY CARDS

HAL ROACH PRESENTS
STAN LAUREL
OLIVER HARDY
IN THEIR NEW FULL-LENGTH FEATURE PICTURE
SONS OF THE DESERT
CHARLEY CHASE

THEIR NEW FULL-LENGTH FEATURE PICTURE
STAN LAUREL
OLIVER HARDY
IN
Sons of the DESERT

THEIR NEW FULL-LENGTH FEATURE PICTURE
STAN LAUREL
OLIVER HARDY
IN
Sons of the DESERT

THEIR NEW FULL-LENGTH FEATURE PICTURE
STAN LAUREL
OLIVER HARDY
IN
Sons of the DESERT

STAN LAUREL · OLIVER HARDY
HAL ROACH PRESENTS
in their new full-length picture
SONS OF THE DESERT
with CHARLEY CHASE
MAE BUSCH
DOROTHY CHRISTY
LUCIEN LITTLEFIELD
DIRECTED BY WILLIAM A. SEITER

Film Classic LOBBY CARDS

STAN
OLIVER
LAUREL ★ HARDY in
SONS OF THE DESERT
A HAL ROACH Production • Released thru FILM CLASSICS

STAN
OLIVER
LAUREL ★ HARDY in
SONS OF THE DESERT
A HAL ROACH Production • Released thru FILM CLASSICS

2222
STAN
LAUREL
OLIVER
HARDY
in
SONS OF THE DESERT
A HAL ROACH Production • Released thru FILM CLASSICS

STAN
LAUREL
OLIVER
HARDY
in
SONS OF THE DESERT
A HAL ROACH Production • Released thru FILM CLASSICS

STAN
OLIVER
LAUREL ★ HARDY in
SONS OF THE DESERT
A HAL ROACH Production • Released thru FILM CLASSICS
COUNTRY OF ORIGIN U. S. A.

STAN
OLIVER
LAUREL ★ HARDY in
SONS OF THE DESERT
A HAL ROACH Production • Released thru FILM CLASSICS
COUNTRY OF ORIGIN U. S. A.

Re-release PRESS SHEET

"Sons of the Desert" does not have Laurel and Hardy as Foreign Legionnaires. They played Legionnaires in the films "Beau Hunks" and in "The Flying Deuces." This later reissue used photo images from "Beau Hunks" and seemed to have confused the two films when creating the ads, probably due to the word "desert" appearing in the title.

PREVIOUS VOLUMES IN THIS SERIES

COMING NOVEMBER 2015

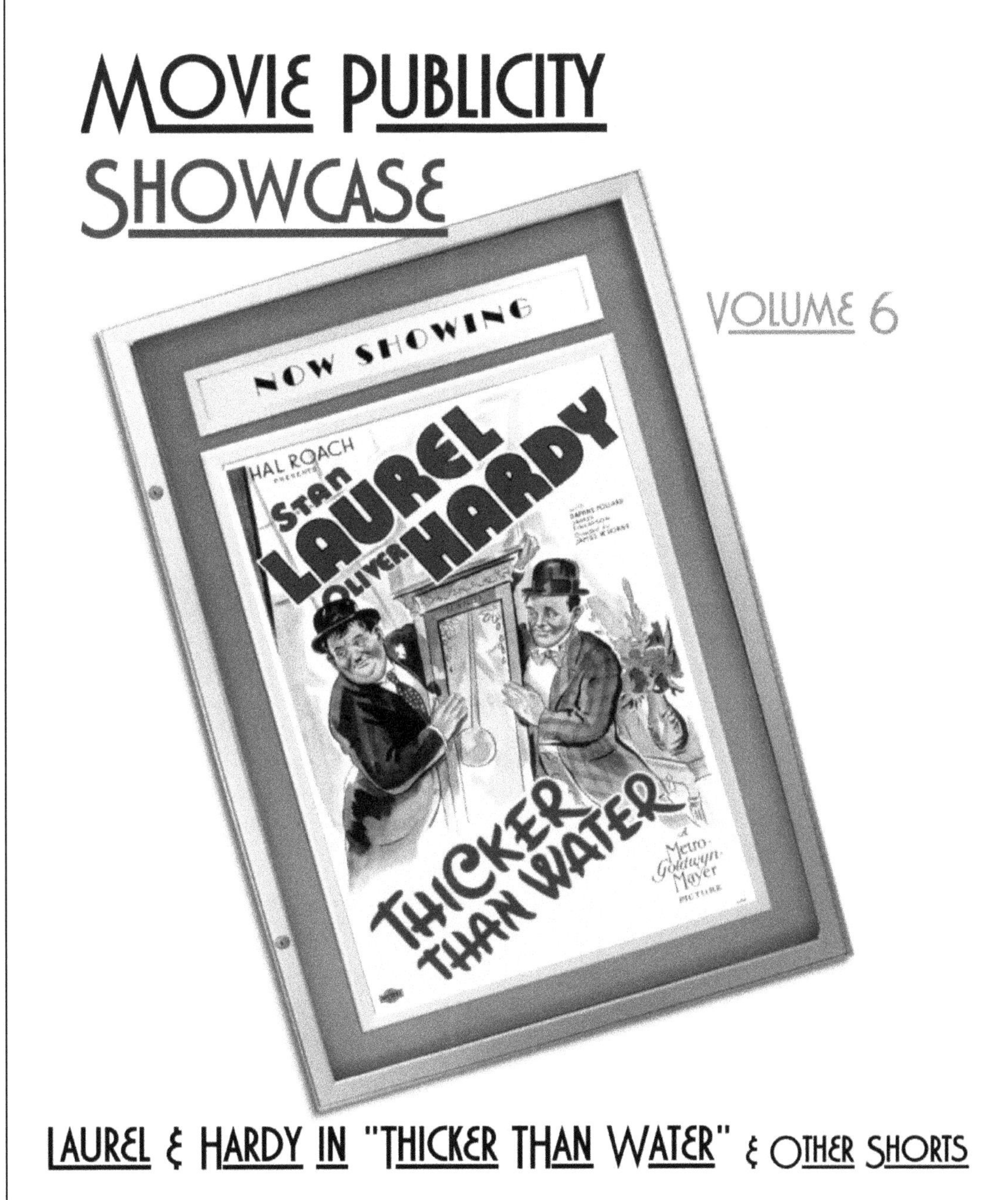

LAUREL & HARDY IN "THICKER THAN WATER" & OTHER SHORTS

BY I. JOSEPH HYATT

ABOUT THE AUTHOR

I. Joseph Hyatt is an entertainment archeologist. A member of the Sons of the Desert, the Laurel and Hardy Appreciation Society, Hyatt's articles have been printed internationally. Traveling across the US, and drawing on many collections, including his own, he brings back past eras with words and photographs.

His first book, "Stan Laurel's Valet - The Jimmy Murphy Story" was based on his close friendship with Jimmy Murphy. While a biography of one of the world's most entertaining valets, it's focus includes the 1940-42 US theatrical tours of Laurel and Hardy.

"Life and Death of a Movie Theater" tells the story of a small town theater and its competition from the depression through the war years, the television years and through to the current day.

He has also written "Hollywood Victory Caravan" which describes the USA's largest bond tour during the war years. Rare private home movie frames capture and recreate the entire show. Travel with the troupe to all 12 cities. Extra information includes the Mexico pre-show and the San Francisco post-show. Souvenir programs from Bob Hope, Oliver Hardy and Charles Boyer are reproduced along with ticket stubs, crew badges, advertising and publicity photos. Stars include (in alphabetical order) Desi Arnaz, Joan Blondell, Joan Bennett, Charles Boyer, James Cagney, Claudette Colbert, Jerry Colonna, Bing Crosby, Olivia de Havilland, Cary Grant, Charlotte Greenwood, Bob Hope (as Master of Ceremonies), Bert Lahr, Frances Langford, Stan Laurel and Oliver Hardy, Groucho Marx, Frank McHugh, Ray Middleton, Merle Oberon, Pat O'Brien, Eleanor Powell, Rise Stevens, and many more! Available in Color or Black and White editions.

Other books by I. Joseph Hyatt:

Movie Publicity Showcase Volume 1: Laurel and Hardy in "Swiss Miss"
Movie Publicity Showcase Volume 2: Laurel and Hardy in "Saps at Sea"
Movie Publicity Showcase Volume 3: Oliver Hardy and Harry Langdon in "Zenobia"
Movie Publicity Showcase Volume 4: Laurel and Hardy in "The Flying Deuces" & "Utopia"
Movie Publicity Showcase Volume 5: Laurel and Hardy in "Sons of the Desert"
Coming in November 2015
Movie Publicity Showcase Volume 6: Laurel and Hardy in "Thicker Than Water" and other short subjects

The Movie Publicity Showcase series places movies into their historical "first run" context, utilizing original press material from the time of their release, and subsequent theatrical revivals. Read about your favorite stars as they were during the day of the movie's initial release. See how creative theater managers could draw in an audience when movie exhibition was an art form. Step back into time and see what movie fans of that day experienced when going to the movies!

www.ingramcontent.com/pod-product-compliance
Ingram Content Group UK Ltd.
Pitfield, Milton Keynes, MK11 3LW, UK
UKHW051135260726
13967UKWH00010B/3062